Milet Publishing
Smallfields Cottage, Cox Green
Rudgwick, Horsham, West Sussex
RH12 3DE England
info@milet.com
www.milet.com
www.milet.co.uk

First English–Chinese edition published by Milet Publishing in 2013

Copyright © Milet Publishing, 2013

ISBN 978 1 84059 790 5

Original Turkish text written by Erdem Seçmen
Translated to English by Alvin Parmar and adapted by Milet

Illustrated by Chris Dittopoulos
Designed by Christangelos Seferiadis

Printed and bound in Turkey by Ertem Matbaası

My Bilingual Book

Sight

看

English–Chinese

Milet

How do we see colors on a butterfly's wings?

我们是如何分辨蝴蝶翅膀的色彩？

Let's think about how we see things . . .

让我们回想如何用双眼看世界。。。

Our eyes show us everything, like faces,

我们的双眼为我们展示周围的一切，例如人们的面庞、

colors, actions, places . . .

肤色、动作和环境。。。

Giraffe has a coat of brown spots on yellow.

长颈鹿黄色的皮肤上遍布褐色的斑点。

Watch him bend to say hello!

你看，他正弯下长长的身躯和你打招呼呢！

Our eyes can show our feelings.

我们的双眸展示着我们的内心感受。

We see Panda's eyes are smiling.

我们看见熊猫的双眼在微笑。

To see, we need more than our eyes.

要欣赏周围的一切，我们需要的不仅仅是双眼。

We need light at night to help us spy.

在夜晚我们还需要光线帮助我们察觉一切。

Owl can see in a different way.

猫头鹰则有着不同的视觉表现方式。

Even in the dark, he can spot his prey.

即便周围漆黑一片，它仍能准确的辨别猎物。

Seeing through glasses? Now I'm perplexed!

透过眼镜看世界？ 现在，我的视线模糊不清！

When our eyes need help, we give them specs!

当我们的双眼需要帮助时，我们可以选择佩戴眼镜！

Tears are not only for sad or happy,

眼泪不仅表示悲伤或喜悦，

they help keep our eyes moist and healthy.

还能帮助我们的双眼保持湿润和健康。

Our eyelids spread our tears when we blink,

眼睑在我们眨眼时扩散眼液，

and we use them to sleep and to wink!

并帮助我们合眼入睡！

We close our eyes when we're asleep in bed,

当我们在床上入睡时闭合双眼，

but in our dreams, we may see orange, green, red . . .

但在梦境中，我们还能看到五彩斑斓的橙色、绿色、红色。。。